www.finishinglinepress.com

# All the Connecting Lights

*poems by*

# Gary Thomas

*Finishing Line Press*
Georgetown, Kentucky

# All the Connecting Lights

Publisher: Leah Huete de Maines
Editor: Christen Kincaid
Cover Art: Sarah Stevenson
Author Photo: Jack Sutton
Cover Design: Elizabeth Maines McCleavy


Order online: www.finishinglinepress.com
             also available on amazon.com

Author inquiries and mail orders:
Finishing Line Press
P. O. Box 1626
Georgetown, Kentucky 40324
U. S. A.

# Table of Contents

## These

## Dyads

*For my father*
*Guy Milton Thomas*
*(1893-1958)*

*and my granddaughter*
*Orly Jane Thomas*
*(born to light)*

# All the Thinking Is About

*(after Robert Hass' "Meditations at Lagunitas")*

All the old thinking is about the night
you figured you would not outlive,
that shame you would never put right,
the damage beyond any dawn's darning.

All the next thinking is about amends
you feared to make to those who might
not forgive, might stare into you and see
who you were, but you know you must try.

All the thinking in this instant is about
what is needed:  barely more than breath,
not quite clever enough yet to form full
sentences, but willing, and without regret.

# Theres

# Oleanders and Whoopee Cushions

There
        between a next-door neighbor's driveway and mine
        between the base of one dusty shrub and another
        among the long-dropped leaves dead as desert cement
this morning as I masked against one toxin
        while trying not to inhale another
        while trying to make sense of something
            fundamental as what's left behind—
              a robin's burst blue egg
              a stiff black widow in her viscous web
              earwigs belly up or ready to boil out at a touch
              sowbugs millipedes undulating plotting their day
              ragged candy wrappers from last Halloween
              weekly shopper news now moot indecipherable
and at bottom
              pale pink as an old eraser or baseball bubble gum
                a genuine JEM brand Whoopee Cushion
                    its bladder split and emptied like an old joke
                        now told to vermin and poison bushes
Of course
all of it went into the green bin for *garden refuse*
along with weeds prunings clippings stuff that refuses to compost
almost a week's worth of what's discarded from what grows or outgrows
alive and fundamental until it isn't a part of what we live with anymore

# Trusting the Songbird Lights

Across the road, five telephone wires
carry crows like whole notes newly strewn
from a bass clef of creosoted Jack pine.
They wait for the next bar, their chance
to scavenge or savage a meal or a squabble,
then sing over it in their antiphonies
of awful joy.
                  Below them, sparrows
manage a morning dust bath on a levee
as they preen and chirrup in concert.
        Red-winged blackbirds, epaulets ablaze,
        plead *Terrr-eeee——*
                Well-removed, polyglot mockingbirds in Fay Elberta trees
                parody these and others' babble, white fantails atwitch
                with the orchard's rhythm.

None of them, nor doves nor meadowlarks, are aware or would care
that I am nearby to watch their movements,
the measures they make their own,
the light around them settling,
nourishing these meager acres
of disk-harrowed soil as I listen
to their songs of desire and need
as I am thirteen in '61.

This humbler morning half a century and a decade later,
a warbler lights on my patio feeder with an urgency
to let the wide world know why he has his name.
By now I know his light is within his wings,
his unknowable throat, that all his fellows share
this radiance, this winged future tense I trust.

# Spring Rationales

In this chill grey instant, we stand stock-still
in the middle of a gravel road, so intent
on a killdeer's egg bare before us
we do not see the others just behind our heels.

We wait inside our abbreviated breaths
for the mother's return, her warning pipe
and broken-wing pretense, her poor defenses
against a parent's absence and our witlessness.

A pond close by buzzes warm from its full day's work.
Every unstudied insect's fleeting wings rest briefly
on the rushes and low branches, then disappear
while we loiter about our obtuse business.

While we look for her elsewhere, she comes back
unbeknownst, distracts us now with her diversion dance
around the air around us, caroming to and from the grit
of her nest, and somehow now we see the eggs all around us.

We are startled, ashamed, ask each other in whispers
as we slink and steal away so we may not rend asunder:
*How could we have known?  Will all these survive?*
*When shall we come back?  How can we ever return?*

We already know the answers,
newly translated from aggregate carvings,
roots, untrampled grasses, widespread shelters.
Other birds call as night begins,

glide and sidle to convene and care
for each other.  We step as carefully
as we can, cross the next road over
as common egrets descend.

# Gospel According to March 28

Wind is how the valley announces spring—
a fulmination of blossoms, bright alms
left at our doorsteps, compassion carried
by the whim and purpose we call blessings.

A fulmination of blossoms, bright alms
to us unworthy mendicants, endowed
by the whim and purpose we call blessings,
intimations of more full-blown bouquets.

To us unworthy mendicants endowed,
entrusted with this season's custody,
intimations of more full-blown bouquets,
this gift as well:  *Gladly bear joy's burden.*

Entrusted with this season's custody
left at our doorsteps, compassion carried,
we take care, considering the lilies.
Wind is how the valley announces spring.

# A Mercantile

*(Dereliquerat for Old Sheep Ranch Store, Calaveras County)*

Rust and rot live in this place
       of give and take, arrivals and exits—
mostly in what men made—
      the corrugated iron roof
           now a neglected skin of cinnabar,
      all the wood once painted white
          become mouldered grey
          or muddy russet—
but also in the river rock façade
       that still fronts the old store
and the gas pump resting
      like a headstone with its
      Visible Glass tank atop,
          its epitaph forever asserting
          *18¢A GAL,*
      where trapped dead flies
          and cobweb filaments
      now displace the petrol,
      long gone to other atmospheres
      and destinations, outlasting
      even the edge-of-town honkytonk
      and out-of-plumb railcar diner.

No one cranks 30-weight
from the Lubesters
on the porch. No one
sits and palavers
on the porch benches.
No one steps onto the porch
to pass through the double doors
in search of fishing tackle
and single cans of Schlitz.

This is the place of oxide
as it settles in,

octane as it atrophies.
Here abide the lost, those
abandoned to swirl among
dust motes, free-range sheep,
and unused memory,
whose textures and traces
might still be familiar and felt,
if only in this moment.

# Shufflebrain

Glenn Gould pedals the pipe organ in my Toyota, followed
by Gram Parsons playing the part of the Grievous Angel
piloting Tom Waits and Iris DeMent to a heaven
orchestrated by Talking Heads as I change lanes
toward the Berkeley exit off 580.  I've shifted frames
of mindfulness a few dozen times as the shades of March green
vibrate themselves into buildings meant to tuck
subtly into the hills, even as a slash of purple,
of yellow or aluminum throbs just behind
a picture window that stares out at the jittery world.
I find myself melding into the landscape of intention and risk,
like a deck of blue Bicycle cards ruffling out its singular wings
in search of just the right Schwinn spokes to perch upon and sing and tap out
an apt spring paradiddle at some juncture between miles per hour
and stream of snapshots—an opera of cracked moments and odd melodies
to purr all the way home from wherever this is, in whatever mind
I am presently motoring toward the next exit or encore.

## A Blur of Walnuts

*at Santa Fe speed*, I start to write, then
realize I meant Amtrak, and that now
I'm a part of the ride that displaced
the dome car with this big brutalist window
that looks down on a plastic dome tent
beneath the Hanford overpass
this Sunday morning.  It occurs to me
in this train-whistle moment
that I am more homeless, but far safer
than the old couple emerging from that
sun-bleached blue tent flap.  I wave off
this guilt as transient terror and summon
a memory of walls of nut orchards suspending
the emerald ornaments of those walnut husks
as they sped into a daze of everything ever unripe.

Now cotton, now dun-colored dust
an hour from Bakersfield, halt
in Corcoran for a dead-stop gaze
at oleanders and decades-old paint,
tumbleweeds trapped in chain-link
time-out pens bordered by crushed
nutshells and rusted Pepsi machines.
Super Chief, I pray, flow easy next to
the canals and wetlands, the corn the corn
the corn and prone alfalfa, aggressive oranges,
peaches *just about* ready for the ladders
and sweat-weary pickers.  Carry me safe
to the next waystation, let me see
how Oildale is holding up.  If I
catch sight of another couple near
another cheap tent, let me be close
enough to lend my hand, give them
a lift up so they can take my seat
and see their own wonders.

# Continuum

This rude round table,
this blue glass cup,
book of poems,
tablet, tan oak leaf
are what my hands
have touched
this morning.

This morning full of vapors,
unfamiliar bird song,
truck engine catching,
visible breath, shivers
are what I have learned
so far about Saturday.

About Saturday is a sheen
made of its own silence,
a holy awareness,
an *I-am-ready,*
a *this-is-plenty* orison
sung in unison
with its kindred days.

# What I Remember of the Gallery

There was a Renoir and a Kandinsky
side by side, and I wondered

what Pierre-Auguste and Wassily would have
to say to each other, whatever else of craft

they might have in common.
I imagine that even with fame,

citizens and comrades
would sometimes thin out,

and there'd be these uncomfortable silences
when no one was watching

or studying or assessing or even
appreciating their art. *Nice blues,*

they could say, *and I like how you
get downright whimsical from time*

*to time*, and then what?
Trane and Bird could say the same thing

to one another, and mention Miles,
how they miss his voice

and scrapper's jab at the valves, and
then what? Puff out their cheeks

like Dizzy, deflate them like Pops,
chuckle huskily, nod, leave

the scene? Which is what I did,
in my way, as I rounded the corner

into the next room full
of nothing but Chagalls

and Pollocks.

# Blitz

*(for London—7 July 2005)*

Bombs fell toward a sky
from underground, wresting blood, soot, faces
from the refuge of earth.  No more warning
than eruptions ever give.  No other claims
beyond what bodies may be found.  No wisdom
but strangers helping each other breathe an air
old as stolen fire.

Moorgate, Aldgate, Liverpool Street,
Edgware, Tavistock,
Russell Square, King's Cross—
names to chant, haunted
in all daylights after this one
by new Rippers, new Reichsführers,
cold, profane, entirely resolved.

Bits of a sentence broken mid-word,
traces of a scarf left on a bus,
scraps of an embrace only begun,
shreds and spots where a morning had started—
Olympus in tatters, Götterdammerung in Hyde Park,
Muhammad weeps in the tube.

# The Whole Town Was Homeless

This was the clock tower
                bell tower
             comm tower
                    water tower
               minaret
where they waited to meet

        This room was where they were after that
        This restroom arch held the huddled strangers from more harm
        This classroom thrived with third graders
                          poets
                          engineers
                          whispers about a paper
                                    a test
                                    an invention
                                    another drill

These were pleated skirts
          sneakers
          ball caps
          balls about to be inflated
          before the bell
                    the klaxon
                          all the metal human sirens sounded in time
                                        or too late
This could have been Amatrice
          Aleppo
          Apalachicola
          This is Anywhere plans and their opposites meet
                              move on even though
                              make Anything human
                                    and in common

# Walking the Hearts from One Place to Another

Ambulance.  Courage.
Flattened.  Flummoxed.

A vocabulary of firestorms—
shrieks of lacerated alloys and limbs,
sirens from mosques, hilltops, sundered parents,
questions pathetic, rhetorical, ignored.

All the news of these muscles—
names of unfamiliar homes,
fly-cars to, full arms from
places where the hearts
had need of deliverance
from defilement.  How
they became hapless.  When
others should start to care.

Walk the wretched sacks of muscle away
from explosion, mudslide, disappeared hospital
since there are no wheels, nowhere to go, really.
No time, no way to parse what makes
one heart carry another somewhere
somehow unscathed, if only
for respite from babel.  Hope is on foot.

Stolid, the rooms where the still hearts are lain.
Tender, the hands that will wash the hearts' husks
if there is time till the next hearts' arrival.
Ardent, the human ambulance as it conveys
the vital cargo each of us could be.

# Staying Lost

*You could like being lost
once you've come this far* —Sekou Sundiata ("Dijerrido")

It was like this—
two trails diverged
in a pine-green glade
and I took the one
less littered with horse
manure.  Colorado
offers its manifold
passages for those
who wish to walk
from park to tundra,
and I was on one
of those.  Intent
on the eventual,
I neglected the current,
the process of sun's
and wind's story,
what the aspen grove
with small grey birds
inside had to say.
By one choice I was
lost, by another I lost
the point of it, by then
I commenced to simper
like some Rocky Mountain
idiot savant who just caught
the punchline to the Cosmic Giggle.
By this means, I found
a way back, listening
to the commonest of
sounds—this grasshopper
whirring his own way across
the trail, that flicker keeping
her drumbeat steady in the
nearest bristlecone, my feet

crunching ineptly on the
duff and granite.  Once
I could see the spot of light
I had started from, I stood still,
looked at it long and easy.
I spun all the way around,
still lost, now liking it, far
from where I had decided
I was headed.  Like that.

# Thens

# And there were birds on the riverbank in 1958,

singing and setting up shop
for the day's business of swooping
and stealing from our orchard
the first fruits, bitter and unforgettable,
thoroughly intoxicating.  And there,
glinting in the first really hot day,
empty white port and tokay bottles,
abandoned on levees, clear evidence
of last summer's harvesting.  Here
and there, I can see where they were—
men who climbed ladders and bent
low, women who were quiet, nursing
babies in old cars, older kids
learning to pick and fill pails, dust
always drifting, clinging to their voices.

And there were dark songs in the morning—
mockingbirds and magpies taunting,
daring the sky to out-sing them, swearing
by all rivers and canals they knew
that this spring was theirs, and there
was no one who could argue, no one
who was not drunk on dawn and ready
to float among trees, choosing the likeliest
peach, the perfect time for songs always there.

## Original Astronomy

I am from the space between
the two largest almond trees
on any farm on Leckron Road,
where I learned to climb
and fall and climb again,
pretending each time
I could fly
and look down at the green shiver
of the leaves, even the birds below me
settling to snack on the unripe almonds.

Since I could not fly, I settled
for teaching my nieces and nephews
to scrape their kneeways
to the top of one tree
while I clambered to the top of the other,
where we would call to each other,
pretending the space between us was planetary
and we, like the almonds, were stars
linked in the constellation
we would name Leckron.

# Two Blinks and You've Passed It

A curse on both your stop signs,
your one-room doll's house of a library,
Rae's Bar with half its neon gasping,
Santa Fe station soon to be demolished,
erasing one more way to leave this place.

School bus, shop class, beggar man's sheaf
of spelling tests, New Math Base 7 homework,
desperate essays on old newsprint:  may you
all go into the same brick campus incinerator
as every mucilage-based hot lunch I gagged
down, be thrice-damned to elementary hell.

Sno-White Burgers, Union 76 station serving
equal amounts of grease and sullen scowls—
all you unlicensed plumberslocksmithsfurniturerestorers
                    antiquedealerslumberyardstrailerparks—
each farmer in the Grange Hall who told a joke about darkies
            when his wife and kids were out of earshot—
the geysers of vapid patriotism spewing from Cub Scout dens
            in the basement of the Church of the Brethren—

You, Town, basis and blight of my childhood, I anathematize you
with unblinking eyes.  May I drive past you—if I ever do again—as though
you are extinct, extinguished, become a pillar of salt and valley dust.

# Canal

I'm seven I think
my father is teaching me how
to walk down the cement steps
covered in green slime and godknows
whatother greasysmutty muck
this reckless valley retches
where I work on my dogpaddle
day after day until I like doing
it        savor the getting somewhere
once I'm there    finally relish
the climb up the slick steps        the view
of vineyards and orchards and beyond
the look back at what I've learned

# life as peaches

take life
as you would
peaches

seize it juicily
down your throat
splitting it in half first
as you would a freestone
or if it's a cling
plunge your teeth
in like fingernails
to grab and shred
and outline the sweetness

let it run down your chin
the stain will be a mark of full high summer

the heat in the dust and fuzz
will ooze wet fine vibrant lushness
like a mirage in your hand
that will linger sticky tacky enough to hold gold
as nuggets atoms waves of heat and syrup
all the sensations of this heavy afternoon
all the gravity you need to get through
all the summers you will savor

# Afterneath

The afternoon broil forced us under
blown branches of dead-ripe peach trees.

We buffed away dust that cloaked each peach,
bit deep, compared the shapes in its flesh.

Leaning back against the levees, ten years old
and the tree ten older, we two were clear as opals—

our eyes saw no further than glimpses of sun
through sleepy leaves and orchard shimmer.

We would have called this *fun* back then,
but *safe* was how we felt before that shelter

became the after we know now neath
the menace in the shadow on this valley.

The peaches are gone, but the fruit
those trees bore is us as we are, not yet

dead ripe, still ready to plant seeds when spring
wheels round, always inclined to hope

that summer will be sweet,
that harvest will serve us all.

# Bent

*I ain't broke but I'm badly bent. —Authorship Uncertain*

Santa Fe tracks roared close by
our farmhouse.  We kids would
plant dull pennies on the rails
hook fast behind a walnut tree
wait till a freight or Super Chief
stamped the coins into razor-thin
saucers or cameos of Lincoln.
The mystery and peril were as vital
as the outcome to us—this was
illegal after all—so we hung around
lied about that double play we could
have turned if only      until the cab
oose's red light winced and squinted
to its pinpoint.  Then we sprinted
to the rails to reap our crushed copper
prizes.  Once we tried a bright new
quarter but it just leapt off the rail
before the wheels and their wind
grumbled past.  One of us crouched
to see the nothing that had happened
and all of us griped we'd been swindled.

Today I practice what it will be like
to harvest pole beans as I stoop to
conquer wee nettles and nut grass
near what will be sprouts and flowers
on their way to my chest-high reach.
In the awakened earth I see some
few contorted ten-penny nails from
back when I whacked this raised bed
roughly together.      Like me and
my favorite garden hand tools
they are cranky rusty reminders
of what can be shaped beyond
breaking to be of use but just

barely      like a coin that no
longer spends but still sparkles
      a body now more prone
to excuses than to taking deep
bows      a day that leans into
an oblique horizon grateful
for the mystery.

## An Absence

I wasn't there when you chose each other,
but I remember you washing dishes
together, mostly without words, how
your hands shared the plates as they rose
from the soapy water, then into the rinse water
on their way to the rack, radiant and steaming.
One of you could have done the whole chore,
of course, but then would have missed
the common silence, the same as when you
read by the cathedral radio tuned to some
concerto from the East, Beethoven's
adagio dialogue between bassoon and piano
surviving the static all the way to the allegro,
when I imagine you looking up from your
*Farm Journal*, your Pearl Buck, and smiling
at the arpeggios, then the cadenza—but I
wasn't there.

## 4th Grade Photo

I am ugly
I am 9 and ugly
I am 9 and ugly in a crewcut
I am 9 and ugly in a crewcut my parents made me get
just before September school pictures were taken

I am scowling
I am scowling to show them and anybody else who is ever forced
to see this school picture tucked inside Christmas cards
my mom insists I sign "to show them you're thinking of them"—
to really show them I am outraged to be more close-shorn
than my dad or older brothers in the pictures of them
in privates' fatigues from that war they call The Big One
I am scowling so that no one will recognize me
I am scowling so that everyone recognizes me and blames my parents
for what's been done to me

I am 9
I am 9 and ugly
getting uglier
Wait'll you see next year's pictures

# Clarinet Lessons

The most salient feature is a good reed,
unchipped, well-wet, accurately positioned,
carefully vibrated.  Because of that, and because
the voice of its cylindrical bore eluded me,
really, I was no good at playing its music.
My mother, however, insisted it was good for me.
My elementary school music teacher,
whose very name sounded like a woodwind,
was a tyrant, demanding tonal perfection
from children not tall enough to sit as straight
as he insisted.

In the tiny room at the music store,
the private teacher my mom swore
could make me a better musician
was alternately bored and punctilious,
but at least he knew that I was
a lousy clarinetist, so we understood each other
and persisted until I moved on to high school,
where other lessons about rhythm, melody,
and disappointment awaited me.

Now I wish I had kept the clarinet,
always snug in its blue velvet, to remind me—
the truest notes we bring forth depend not on skill,
but a desire to make our reeds quiver a music alive.
In this way, we register the world's resonance
and become its instruments, its choir
of clarinets, its Klezmer chorale, its Bartok Bebop
barbershop quartets.  Listen—you will hear a family
playing all its voices, abject or angelic, finally knowing
what is good for us—a true ensemble best in B flat.

# Deuce Stick

6th grade teacher with the name like trauma
hung it from an 8-penny nail

next to the blackboard with 3 yellow chalks
made from the ground bones of 35 students.

*2 feet long and hurts like the devil—*
his way of advertising the upcoming

to us just before 1 of us,
doubled over a desk, got it:

the thwack, the wallop
from the special blonde ruler

made of Louisville Slugger ash,
repeated 10 echoes' worth,

preparing us for each day's deuce stick,
double whammy, special report,

duplicate memo, binary code
we get now.   Only I never learned

whatever math problems I needed
to know in 7th grade, so I have trouble

counting the number of times
we are hurt, especially in centimeters.

# Oak Bow Education

The arrows I knew when I was eight
were made by my father from leftover flooring,
extra tongue-and-groove scantlings, dense planks
of oak and maple, and as he sawed them thin
and whittled them round and smooth, I breathed in
the redolence of their grains and his labor,
knowing that each was being fashioned for me alone,
that he would fletch and notch the nether ends
with jay feathers and great care,
sharpen and varnish the business ends,
as he called them, each finished shaft
mine to aim and find the center of hay bales
or lose in the weeds beyond.

From this I learned, of course,
craft and responsibility, which were
the real points, and when he turned his hand
to the shaping of a bow selected
from the same woods, showing me how
he glued alternating strips of oak and maple,
let them set and cure all day, then planed them,
the curls and coils collecting on the sawdusted floor,
followed by finer carving and notching,
showed me how to brace the finished bow
properly with the buckskin bowstring
braided from a discarded bridle,
let me make the maiden pull and aim and détente,
I learned the next lesson of a father's love—
the creation of the useful,
followed by the letting go.

# Integers

When I was eight, it was the law:
*Count to ten if you are angry;*
*you might say something*
*you can never take back.*

It was my introduction to higher mathematics—
I learned to count very rapidly,
and how the numerals looked in my head
as I called their names,
subtracted the fury,
unballed my fists
digit by digit.

Before I could multiply
or imagine a table
as anything other than a place
for grace and pancakes,
before long division and remainders,
I learned to calculate
how long it would take
my enemies to turn to ciphers,
my losses to lessons,
and that 10 equaled X,

which marked the spot my brothers stood
where the school bus dropped me that December day
they told me about our father.
For the first time, I counted to twenty, twice as slow,
half as loud as I had ever heard him whisper my name
or his favorite psalm as it was read three days later,
as I tallied tiny holes in the chapel's ceiling tiles,
keeping quiet, acquainting myself
with the algorithms of loss.

And tonight I wait to tell you I love you,
canceling any arithmetic I ever memorized
or put to practical use. This is something else

I can never take back:
together we will be divisible
only by each other,
and counting:
1...

# The morning of my middle brother's funeral,

wind chimes woke me, followed by
a rattle of tiny white Christmas lights
against a brimming rain gutter,
a storm announcing itself.

Today soldiers will shoot guns
twenty-one times over the body of my brother
sometime between ten-thirty and eleven hundred—
Army time to the end.

Later will be food prepared by ladies from the circle,
another service in a stern brick church
with kin and other survivors weeping,
scavenging for some words that make sense.

then more food shared,
words we speak through the code of grief,
some laughter over some joke he'd told
long ago or the last time he could,

then some long dry silences
punctuated by other strings of lights
rattling their own code,
deciphering the storm.

All I can hear now are wind chimes,
the way we all know this music
of gaps between notes,
a duet of air and earth.

# On Being Caught and Falling Down

*The spirit catches you and you fall down.*
(Hmong explanation of epilepsy)


Tickle,
tremor,
tongue still,

eyes swallow
all they see inside,
all that lights the outside.

First hits, whiffs
of adolescence—
my full share

of *grand mal* seizures,
unseemly treatments,
electroshock sessions

with the bit in my teeth,
a quack psychiatrist
scratching cold notes,

winding down to *petit mal*—
lightheaded a minute a month or so,
and so passing through

to the episode this morning—
unlike youth, not blacking out
or seizing, more like stepping

into grand waves of grey electricity,
someone picking me up by the shoulders,
rotating me gently, horizontally,

three hundred sixty clear degrees,
so I can see all around me.

It gets my full attention.
In a moment, things gone dormant
awaken, headline already attached:
*Seizure Shakes Hands with Satori,*

and I am livid because I do not want
to fall down that rabbit hole again,
do not want to relearn the lesson
that will save me from my selves—
the alerted, the startled,
the irate, the sedated.

But I relent at last and bring
this epileptic news from one
who has been caught too often—

We abandon as much of the anger
as we can stand and still live,
fear and resentment at lips' gates,

let gods play their parts,
make some sense of it all, then
doze clear through the night,

as if nothing had occurred,
as though only sleep had caught us
and morning would always arrive.

# These

# Arrayed Like These

I.

Exhausted, the little owls
still hunger in their ugliness
for what their mother cannot provide,
their nest so close to the runway
when they were yet unhatched,
their shells throbbing to the ascending engines.

II.

Snoring, aunt and nephews slump to starboard
in the Union Station narthex,
bide each other's time,
provide what can be shared,
close to the gate where they will awaken,
souls on track and all aboard.

III.

Shivering, the old sloth
shelters himself in the baobab,
veldt filling with monsoon swell—
knowing providence is in precision,
he takes his time, and some other sloth's.
Now sated, he races imperceptibly home.

IV.

Expectant, the attorney
sends out for sushi, hopes
his children enjoy the exotica of eel,
postpones the news of the new provider,
the one his wife took her time to find:
steady, stay-at-home, un-him.

V.

Undecided, the razor clam
stays put, hydraulics on call,
bivalved, bigenderous, empties
what must be expelled into larger seas,
then like a sigh, carries home away,
escapes entire to the unknown provided.

# Even This Day

*If a Poem Can Be Headed into Its Proper Current*
*Someone Will Take It Within His Heart*
*to the Power and Beauty of Everybody* —Kenneth Patchen

But before that happens,
we will sit in lines of six,
all facing the front, our eyes focused
on our booklets, our sheets with small circles,
our pencils grinding pock marks hard
into the faces of our desks.

We will pretend for familiarity's sake
that any of this matters,
that our time is well spent,
that if we were to connect the dots,
a poem about architecture would appear,
perfect in its geometry and reason,
beautiful and strong as a cathedral,
a cataract of stone and holy water.

Anyone reading this after we have done breathing
should know we were as alive as if we had been singing
or drifting on small rafts, heading downstream,
staring straight above at all the connecting lights.

# How This Is Poison, Then Isn't

Unkind, our lot,
impure, our ilk.
We oversugar our savories,
our caress envenoms.
We yearn to devour
what cannot be contained
once constrained
and call this pleasure.
Engorged on brightest nettles,
we savage what we say
we would revere.
Somewhat later, honeybees emerge
to sip the liquor that was us.

# From Here (An Ambrotype)

We stay still, unsmiling as the reeking glass plate
reveals us slowly upside down before we return
to our upright daily chores, prepare for the chores after that
for the rest of the day until the rest night brings.
From here, after this, we will forget this was done,
leave it for unknowable others to find in a trunk
filled with the tools and toys of our lives' times.
Maybe they will smile at our dour dull countenances,
wonder how we endured our stiff starched gabardine and linen,
never knowing how we laughed in relief
just after, sat down to our plain supper
of biscuits and beans and cold melon
from the creek, how we became
more than sepia can show, how
we came to create our smiles
still on their faces.

# Near Futures

*We're all driving rocket ships and talking with our minds*
*and wearing turquoise jewelry standing in soup lines.*
  *—John Prine, "Living in the Future"*


We will meet at the coffee shop and talk for two
    full hours
            cook supper for the crowd jostling at the dining room table
              with both leaves added
                        some will help their next-door neighbors
                              fix flats on their kids' bicycles
                                in the cracked driveway
The rest of us will remember a year we learned new definitions of *shelter* and *place*

We will gather in a park for the holoflicks and High Tea brand cocktails
    then float home
              hold a thumb in front of the Random Choice selectscreen
          and pray for steak
                          some might donate to the
                                Agency for Altruistic
                                  Teleschools
The rest of us will remember reciting a poem in what was called junior high English

We will close our eyes to see sports because we have the ability
    and implants are easier than attendance
                        swallow what we are served today by
                            Comprehensive Devices
                                      some
                                      might
                                      share
The rest of us will remember a time we loved madly and held creation close

# Canoe Launch with Bassoon Accompaniment

Whatever the nautical term is—other than *landlubbers*—
for *we-who-rarely-paddle-canoes,* we sure are *that* this morning.

We wear the obligatory gonna-get-wet shorts and ugly-
as-neon-sin lifejackets. We slather our faces, arms, legs

with Neutrogena double-plus-good sun-block, forgetting
the tops of our ears, a couple spots where we flex ankles.

We put anything valuable or actually useful—binoculars,
bird books, camera, spare socks—in the neoprene dry sacks.

We grunt and heft the red three-man canoe christened
*Easy Rider* down the small hill onto the kelp-slick rock jags

and into the water. One of us three actually knows
what he's doing, and tutors us in How and When and Where

to step into a canoe, and we actually don't even come close
to falling in. Before either of us other two can believe

all this is actually happening, we are *rowing in the right direction,*
our paddles stabbing salt water, raking it past us, rising

to repeat, officially On Our Way, eager to Get There. Just
as thoughts of hillbilly mutant banjo music begin to catfish

their way in my skull, I hear, instead, a bassoon in the distance,
double reed running the scales, riding its own waves up and down,

then pushing off into something baroque and deeply beautiful,
an extra nudge for us all, just as our muscles start to whine

and the mystery of where we are, how we move, why we can do this
is clear as a sky full of eagles announcing the beginning of light.

## Ardea

She is called common,
an occupant of marsh and low sky,
plainly white, merely graceful,
her S of a neck and silent flight
the sole reasons for our attention.

But look:  she stretches, stands slack,
then stiff-necked, stirs
the reedy saucepan of the slough,
spears her suppers from all that swims—
a feathery ballet of need, poise, consummation.

She balances her days
as if walking through still water
were as wondrous as walking on it.
She leaves not a ripple,
her reflection the only evidence of motion.
She rises, reaching for her other homes.

She is well-traveled, wintering
in Malawi, lazing in Malaysia,
taking in the taste of unbordered air,
taking her place in the ancient dance,
a gypsy of wind and moment.

# And to the Young Ravens When They Cry
### *(after Psalm 147:1-9)*

September, a Tuesday.  She scatters seeds
from sunflowers that volunteered
for duty next season.  After they
have been lavish, are browned,
will blacken soon, she beheads them,
plunks them on bare ground
behind the lemon tree.  Whatever the ravens
don't extract as they *prruk-prruk-prruk*
in all their ferocity—there is a reason
they are called *ravenous*—will fall away,
be scuffled under
by her feet and garden fork
to be impeccably dormant, break free
and rise, become its strange new self.

The ravens will return, will recruit
the young to cry and call, consider
themselves as they open
their odd wings as they swallow
what was given the season before,
as they praise the yonder
and play tricks.  She
smiles, mulls how she might
clear more ground,
plant more seeds.

## Return to Sender

The sisters told me
*Once there was a letter / No, let me tell him*
*addressed to Resident / Wasn't it Occupant*
*with our address / with our address*
*scratched by a course hand / block-printed, really*
*The return address was a P. O. box / all the way from Oregon*
*and the stamp / yes the stamp was from when*
*you could mail a letter for 3 cents / then 4*
Did you open it I asked
*O yes / soon as we brought it inside*
*with Mama's paring knife / she would've killed us*
*the envelope was a little bulgy / rounded outward she means*
What was inside
*You may not credit this / No*
*but it was just a shell / like a tiny spiral*
*and a bit of beach glass green as 7-Up / shaped like a cameo*
No message?
*That's the thing / We thought about it*
*a long time / till we came to believe*
*these specks / were the message*
*like a memory of a time / and place*
*we would've known down to our kids' souls / if we hadn't been raised in Omaha*
Do you still have it?
*What / the glass / the shell / the envelope*

*No just the picture in our minds/*
*and our West Coast husbands*

# Daughters of the American Revolution Visit the Garden of Gethsemane Church of God in Christ, Mount Rainier, Maryland

Bumper sticker meets church marquee—

*God, Home, and Country*
                    *ATM Inside...Atonement, Truth, and Mercy*

Well-bred flag-blue Ford Fusion parks one door down
from this brick exhorter house of worship.  Waiting
to be winked at, warned, or welcomed, the Ladies emerge
like patriotic mummers, Coach clutches at the ready,
baptism Bibles tucked inside in case anybody asks at the steps
if this is a field trip for the Daughters or something else.
Demure, they glide inside, demur at the offer of a bulletin,
take the right-back pew.  The first hymn starts, something
they know: "Where You Go, I'll Go" and they join in reedily,
following the words on the screen above the altar, but can't
quite remember *all* the chord changes, especially the bridge,
so surreptitiously the five of them leaf through the purple hymnal
till they locate the chorus:
            *Where You go I go*
            *What You say I say*
            *What You pray I pray...*
each silently searching herself, finding she finds herself wanting
the conviction inside the words, but still feebly lifts her voice,
hopes the noise she makes is a joyful one and that the congregants
will forgive her lack of flats and sharps where they should land.
Atonement, they know, takes a long time, and has taken them here,
these daughters of mothers who denied the truth of mercy
to Marian Anderson. They stay for the second hymn, the second
scripture reading led by the Elder who will preach the sermon,
who will shake their hands on their way out.  As if led by some spirit
new to them, they each mark the passage in their Bibles—
Galatians 5:22-23: *But the fruit of the Spirit is love, joy, peace, forbearance,*
*kindness, goodness, faithfulness, gentleness and self-control. Against such things*
*there is no law.*

## While Looking for Levee Breaks, He Leans on His Shovel and Does This—

Reaching with a lazy man's reach
for the nearest lowest limb,
finding a ripe one,
he cradles the peach finally,
firmly as a decision held for years.

He presses in,
feels the give and juice
beneath the furry skin,
beneath the nap like suede,
smells the real ghost in the machine—
no stranger or less mechanized
than a clockwork orange.

He finds the engine of the peach,
the generator of all future fruitions.
He frees this stone clinging for life
to the red strings of flesh.

He flings it into standing water
warm inside levees where it will find
its promise—
a lazy land,
a muddy hand
reaching home,
the soil and the sky.

# That Guy
### (for Rondo Hatton, et. al.)


My shadow leaks from the wall to the floor of some dingy flat,
rounds a corner just enough for you to see my chin from
a central-casting villain vault, then the brow big as the back
of a haunted barn, then my carbon-steel eyes (even in those
'30's and '40's black and white B movies shot in a week
and now remastered, they still glint like switchblade case knives).

Of *course* you remember me, though only
one in a hundred of you remembers any
of my names—it was my *job* to terrify you,
else I wouldn't get asked to shoot a sequel.

I get paid because of how I look, and how
I look is caused by a condition that I
have trouble pronouncing even now—
*acromegaly* could even be my villain's name,
my fellow actors tell me with a wink that says
*Tough luck, Pal, glad I ain't got what you got.*

They neglect to notice my heart, which
will likely kill me tomorrow, next week,
or a couple years from now, on set,
doing my best to make audiences' hearts
shudder at the sight of me.

# Stage Left

*Our revels now are ended*, we might have said
if we'd had the time and allowed ourselves
to believe that, but we didn't and we don't.

What we did was strike the set, rack the props,
mop the floors, lock the stubborn doors for now.
We are a community of characters, and part of

another that needs us to wait in the wings awhile
until all the curtains we're using can be raised.
Past seasons' ghosts stand ready for their cues.

Willy Loman waits to be told he's been let go.
Tom Joad will learn how long dust takes to settle.
Didi and Gogo stand by a bare tree, can't go on, go on.

We learn our parts as yet unwritten, imagine this apron
as fourth wall, try not to bump into makeshift furniture.
We are such stuff.  All the world's a green room now.

# Mister

He said
*Whatchou doin' with what you have*
*where you are?*
I said
*The best I can*
*how I am.*
He said
*You sure you know when*
*that's enough?*
I said
*Never. That's why*
*I keep You so busy.*

# What Will Soon Be the Moon

This is hard work:
losing sight of the sun,
living off reflected light,
keeping steady unto dawn.

I have been worshipped,
blamed, even rhymed,
lost, renewed, not really risen,
just appearing as a reminder.

Hanging on by a fingernail
or holding a muskmelon's gravity,
I do my best to be invisible
till the evening cries *a b r a c a d a b r a* …

Keeping steady unto dawn,
living off reflected light,
losing sight of the sun—
this is hard work.

# Charlie's Maine Autobiography

Flat-top kids near the hospital corner
call me Taxi because my ears are wide
as Checker doors and open for what departs
and what might enter, and I am quick.

Even when I step down from the bus each morning,
I am just a blur with ears protruding,
not so keen as I might be by afternoon rounds,
but there are things I notice.

This evening, lighthouses all down this state's shoreline
will whisper to each other. The heavy ships are waiting
to catch off-color comments in between
the ones that keep them safe and in sight of buoys.

Walking off work just at five, I can close my eyes
and the war is over. All I hear is a slow stammer
of waves in a harbor growing soft and flabby with dusk
as all the light in this unscathed city murmurs itself to sleep.

I outlived it—the darkness, the beach surging with bodies,
my name still in their mouths as words washed away.
I could not get to them as they shrieked and cursed
and trusted me to stop their tide going out forever.

I never wanted to be near saltwater again, but I came here.
I can still heal some—even delivered a baby during a brownout—
and am as healthy as anyone with *Semper Fi* on their left biceps
has any right to be. All the story I have is what I hear in my head.

# Marcel Marceau at the Open Mic

They are used to reading their work this way, these young poets who brandish their splintered screens scarcely containing their need to read what they tapped ten minutes before taking the stage. The more rehearsed read their Anne Frank raps, their epistolary anger poems with air-stabs and Emily references to the one or ones who abandoned them, including their muses, their rhymes coiled into snaky couplets, defiant and proud enough to say *Thank you* when they're done. Some of them forget there's a microphone in front of and not surrounding them, their shock-words that shout become mummery, or alternate between FULL-ON and LOST TO THE ETHER. To clap or to finger-snap? That was the poem.

And I, the elder who appears to chide and be snide and glib enough to ad-lib my years as if I were not this old because I was that young— I was *their* young words once, just without a screen to wield or a stage to take over, *their* visions of justice and the candor to carry them out, only I didn't, enough, and my poems are as long as my time here isn't, and *this* poem wants to say to them: Your Voice is worth your best words, if you can truly believe that, if you can stand to listen to mine, and finally-for-now, I promise I will listen deep for yours, then some more again.

# Dyads

# Neruda and my mother

*—for Neftali Ricardo Reyes y Basoalto and Beulah Belle Talley Thomas*

would be one hundred eighteen today,
sharing, I think, a bowl of fresh peaches
sprinkled with sugar, strewn with cinnamon,
a little milk on top for more comfort.

He would understand her smooth skin,
her full smile ready to sing an old hymn.
She would never fathom his poems or whiskey voice,
but would love his Chilean sun and beaches.

They could talk of children and the sea,
look at old photographs of inner tubes and cousins
floating belly up in afternoon rivers,

learn magic words like *Wichita* and *Santiago,*
write them down with the other bits
of each other's addresses
and promise to write,

and they would, I know,
if only Neruda and my mother
had met on a cruise in 1924,
traveling to Rangoon, Singapore, Batavia,
sleeping on deck to duck the heat,
feeling the breeze and its gift of salt.

Every time the summer sweat
coursed down their lips in all the years after,
they would remember the salt
while they thought of the sweet
peaches and vowels reuniting someday.

# Mr. Erwin, Room 204

Ethel, when I die,
you can sell the berry vineyards
as long as you get a good price.
I'll write down some figures for you
before you leave.  You don't need
to stay much longer.  I know this room
makes you sad, partly because I will die in it
and partly because it doesn't meet your standards
of cleanliness, even as a hospital,
but mostly because you are frightened
by me and the shrunken reminder
of what I used to be:
your husband, companion for forty-nine years
of forgetting forty-nine years as anything more
than a string of days moving together,
leading to this one,
where I look at scalded bushes shaped into green boxes
next to the parking lot, and think of boysenberries
bulging, seedy, staining my fingers and lips and yours,
when we were the only pickers we could afford,
when we still could make a living on twenty acres,
and we were in love, we were,
up to our noses
in purple seedy love,
and we did not know we were
going to be here today.

Tomorrow when you come,
don't talk of the vineyard,
don't need me to talk.
Don't bring anything
that reminds you of anything
except our purple tongues when we kissed
as we moved together
after the harvest.

# Bride of the Butcher, March 1934

*(for Hattie and George Schultz)*

They walk home from the chapel,
pause long enough for the Brownie
to do its plain work.  They pose on the sidewalk
in front of the first and last house they will ever live in.
*Click*—the trees behind them stop
waggling their strange nude arms in the wind.

They are pleased with themselves,
the way they have just married,
with what they are wearing:
simple and pearl grey,
smiling in dark brown.
Her hat is scarlet, though,
low and tilted just so to the side;
his homburg's high band holds a crimson feather.

His arm is around her waist
where it belongs now,
his frank-sized fingers framing her,
making them one flesh truly.
Her hands keep her pocketbook casually close
in front of her, as if their futures were inside its kidskin,
needing her touch, his protection, to have and hold.

Monday he will cut the meat
others will hoard or ration or covet.
They will wonder if his huge thumb
is as thick and heavy as his German tongue
pronouncing the honest price of a porterhouse.
That same morning she will go to the bank,
tell them her last name has changed to *Schultz,*
surprising herself how proud she is,
how good it feels to say her new name
out loud to strangers.

Tonight he calls her *Honey*; she calls him *Unk*.
The wind catches the bedroom door,
pushing it toward them with a *click*.

# After the Epithalamium

We had a big breakfast, as I recall.
Some buttermilk pancakes,
real sausage, truly fried eggs,
orange juice so cold
we each shivered at the first sip,
wanted madly to warm our lips
on each other's risen flesh.  Coffee
the way we never drank it again—
straight black, straight back,
bitter, honestly bad.
We could still sing then, of course,
mostly in tune and a harmony
we fashioned for each other,
trying so hard to smile, remembering
any wedding, any love song
we had bedded by
before.

# Lux

Finding our broken way
home, we found the flashlight
your father loaned us
rusted, in need of new batteries,
black and heavy as our doubts
about the trail through slender moonlight.

We were lost, after all
these years knowing these footpaths.
*All right, we can manage,*
we told ourselves, despite the smirk
your father gave us with the torch
all those rusty dozens of years ago.

The candles came twelve to a box,
and we lost some, didn't we—
and we bought more, didn't we—
and our boys never knew a birthday without candles,
without hearing the longest song in the world
and being reminded they were dear to us.

Then came the year the cake smoke rose,
when we stumbled to the switch plate
and the bulb barked, all its allotted light spent.

Only the full moon led us to the matches on the mantle,
the sullen flashlight meanwhile in a drawer,
feeling cheap, dismissed, unremembered.

We found another bulb nestled beside the loaned light.
We tried it, found it bright enough for another birthday,
another reason to celebrate by extinguishing flames.
Earlier this year we let them burn without a birthday,
lined up along the windowsill, the ones we had left,
the trick kind you can't blow out, even if you wanted.

On a whim tonight we walk outside,
another moon-bright evening, down to the canal,
side by side and nearly silent, familiar
with our imagined faces, carrying the flashlight,
hoping it will be enough,
carrying a votive if it isn't,
finding the path by beam and flame,
using all the light we have,
finding our broken way.

# Galluses

The poke and dandelions huddle near the squash and bush beans, and I let them. Their leaves are wilting, hunching like these shoulders of mine in this August heat. I was going to say *like my trousers,* but today I'm wearing both my belt and galluses, so they don't. I've worn the same Red Wing boots so long they conjure up the gnarled zucchini logs I always find hidden under the farthest leaves a week too late to do anybody any good except the hogs. Once I fell off a fence rail I was perched on and landed ankle deep in their trough slops. That was the end of my perching. That was also when Edna pulled me up and out by my galluses and kept holding me up until '29, when the country and our marriage came undone—nothing to hold us up anymore.

A farmer needs good land, good work to do. A farmer's wife needs her farmer to be true, grow along with her. I wasn't and I didn't. And now I just tend this half acre in an Alabama autumn, thinking of poke salad and dandelion slaw, how she used to put then on our table, head held high.

# A Valediction

We decided to take the long way round
this blighted wilting mining town
so as not to risk the sinkholes
near the nodding courthouse dead center
in the square.  Weary mugwort sprang
from the cracks of every surface once paved,
grey reminders of the blown roses
we once planted in our rock garden—
or so we called it, though all it was
was a border of slag and riprap
round rows of poke and cannas,
carrots and sad petunias.

One last time round our past lives'
birthing rooms, back when
breathing room was a companion,
not a craving,
the long way out of what needs leaving,
advancing toward a horizon
built of coming up short.

# The Oculist

She studies him, especially
how he blinks as he tries
to translate the menu.
She studies him beneath
the cornea of his flattery
as he praises her choice
of Malbec to pair with
his choice of Manchego.
She studies his irises,
how they are never quite
hazel in any light, especially
in the shadowy candles
of this overblown bistro.
She studies herself, especially
how her soul's retina reverses
itself whenever anyone comes
too close. *He is only a man,*
*this is only a first date, we are*
*only as lonely as our vision*
*of our chances to expand beyond*
*this flickering.* She studies
the check as it arrives from
the dusk after dessert, extends
her hand, finds it settling on his.
In each other's silhouettes, they
regard how some new aperture
is opening, something worthy
of consideration, like the first
long gaze into reflected light.

# I Do Not Want to Tell This Joke

But you had to ask.
How many Irishmen make up a village?
No, that's not it.
What do you call an Irishman with an IQ of 140?
Yes, that's it.  A village.

I do not wish to tell this one, either,
but I've been having to ask myself.
How long can one woman
stand a husband of Irish ancestry?
You know:  depends on the husband.
Depends on the length.
Depends on the woman's stand
on other matters.
So the punch line is never
as satisfactory as the set-up.
It takes an Irishman to raise a village.
No, that's not it.
What does it take for a woman
to leave a village?  This Irishman.

## As You Were—

*If I were the man you wanted,*
*I would not be the man that I am.* —Lyle Lovett

—So I will not be.  I won't
make the mistakes you require of me
any longer.  I am done with all
the in-advance apologia you love,
the future regrets I've burnished
and buffed over so many seasons,
glossing over any elation I might
have allowed my soul.
No.  Just no, and while I'm at it,
here's what else:  I surrender
to hope, that stranger, and will play
the good host to her siblings as well,
bid them abide with me.  As I am
become older than the trail I chose,
you will forgive me my new truth,
and consider whether you want me
still, man that I am, wanting you
as much as can be.

# Invocation to the Poet (*Anrufung des Dichters*)
### —*for Lisel Mueller*


Let X stand for a spot we knelt together, prayed to a tumbling river
In late afternoon, then crossed to the other side of how we touched.
Stipple our skin with the time that took, followed by our headlong
Escape to our different memories.  You gave heed to mortal wilds,
Listened deep.   Your mother's death hurt you into poetry, you said.

Mention me later if you wish as just another soul who wakened to words
Untranslatable as light at odd angles and found a home to go to.  You
Explored enigmas of our selves as other souls seeking common time.
Live together, you said, unfurled our hearts' vocabulary in four syllables.
Love songs saved even in a heartless age are at hand.  We can write more.
Every life spans canyons.  Dreaming, we are other secret protean creatures.
Remind me by your words to dance on the bridge as I wait out this storm.

# A Certain Amount of Shredding

This is not a sloughing off,
a whittling down to purity.
This is wholesale ruination,
or at best, future compost.

These are bills paid, bills unpaid,
shopping lists and coupon books,
ads for new gym memberships,
implausible mortgage rates

coaxed sheet by sheets into
the thin maw of a machine
whose one purpose is to turn
twenty pounds of trash into

twenty pounds of trash.  This is
how we show all our intentions:
strip-cut, cross-cut, pygmy-minced
piles of print and pulp.  This is

how we display our papier mâché
faces, wearing our masks so assertively,
having chewed what we could not digest
into our sorrowful and incendiary armor.

# The MacBeths at Home

Woolite won't touch
all the taints of one week,

let alone the fecund laundry
a couple can rip through

in the course of a marriage
barren of anything but style

and timely intrigues.  Milk
and blood pudding are served

as a morning repast or late
night snack— reminders of

some weird sisters' hell-broth
cauldroned from gibbet grease,

goat's gall, Turk's tongue, Tartar's
lips, and other unsavories.

Now come their conversations
of his career advancement, unuttered

palaver on her nocturnal perambulation,
restless silence, then candlelit monologues

on pallid countenance, hand-related hygiene,
foreign fragrances, negligees, and at last,

the should-haves before the hereafters,
too many brief tapers, poor performers,

so much racket, rage, the end of the story,
too late even to beg the grace of Grace.

# The Many Brides of the Monsters

Frankenstein's creature is loose, his bride looser
than the necktie he sometimes affects,
or the bolts in his neck she loves to unscrew
when he comes, calling *Bride good*
in his best basso profundo
bordering on castrato contralto.

Dracula's first wife knew how
his tastes ran to black and red,
so wore those hues exclusively,
sketching concentric circles
around those two precious punctures
through her jugular. *You've got to
keep things fresh*, she assured the next wife,
*or it won't last.*

Larry Talbot's fiancée found his chest hair fascinating,
especially the way it spread all the way
to his ear tops and toenails on those special nights
when noisy sex was not only obligatory, but adorable.

And now, my beloved, let us hasten
to a cool dark place filled with electricity
and a ceiling engraved with full moons,
pledge our troths, say our vows, discover
how alive we can be.

## Durerea este un vampire curios

Pain is one curious vampire, seeking
this knuckle, searing that last nerve.  Elsewhere,
it severs a lover from another
one acute absence or suckling distrust
at a go.  Oh, and Pain's odd retinue—
isolation, avoidance, shivers of
masochism, and what used to be called
*hysteria.  What about Fear*, you ask,
but that's an origin of suffering,
not just another fawning member of
Nosferatu's entourage.  Threats of pain
can be as bad as the bite.  Look into
your friends' faces as they wince.  Can you tell
the wellspring of their distress, or summon
amazing remedies?  Even Grace may
be a creature comprised of twin shadows
at mirrors.  Remember the second verse
of that old hymn: *'Twas grace that taught my heart
to fear, / And grace my fears relieved.*  Just now
as you think of your own pain's synergy,
you conjure an image of a threshold
which we are always approaching, standing
on, or crossing— although vampires have to
be asked to enter, yes?  Your jugular
is precious enough to refuse access,
your heart has a homeowner's right to yank
its welcome mat even if the ghoulish
trespasser has a dismal foot on it.
Panic attacks us all acutely, wounds
arrive peripherally, centrally,
in ordinary sunlight or blood moon,
reading our bodies and spirits like charts.
Ready or not, we half-know our no-self
theory cannot accommodate such
surveillance and damages.  Misery
is personal right down to dark muscle
memory, and loves our company.  Pain's

curiosity shapes our own as we
blithely drain our days with our perfect fangs,
shunning light, swallowed by a pallid night.
Dracula himself knew this, used it to
tantalize Mina: that love, not a thirst
for knowledge of whatever lies beyond
pain, is the light of all lights all our days.

# Reshaping Meringue

We were walking through rooms
of castles we'd built in the exosphere,
using metaphors as patio furniture,
unaware we'd stripped the threads,
that *some assembly required*
meant just finger-tight, no more.

*I never learned to bake,*
you complained, *and I miss it.*
I wondered how you miss something
you never learned, then remembered
how much I've always wanted
to sing in tune, and can't—
I miss that, too.

Egg whites and sugar
beaten stiff as a Haitian drum—let's
let ourselves do the pie dance,
worry about what beads up
later.

# Levain

      1.

Four days for the wild yeasts to be coaxed
by plain flour    fresh water into bubbles

    the aroma of vinegar and belt leather
Then casting away of most of it    more

flour and water to feed it    another day or
two as it doubles    trebles    resembles

something preternatural    protoplasmic    even
neonatal    until the oven reaches 400 and

the oven's maw opens to accept our oblation
of the ordinary    Patience truly begins when

the door shuts and a new fragrance arises like
whole wheat prayer    We make sure the butter

is sufficient for the next ceremonies of coming forth:
admiration blended with wonder for the advent of

two loaves cooling    the long knife as it slices our
common nourishment    steam still exhaling as proof

that this life continues    that what we spread now
extends this small plain sign of grace

      2.

A few days for the wild virus to catch and cling
to the creatures who fed it    the odor of fear

as the new year casts away the first casualties
    us and what we thought we knew of what

we should do     not fight or flight this time
but the real or the rumors broadcast

masked mating calls of jingoes     patrioteers     other
scoundrels whose gullets scourge the truth with their heat

    but miss the plague     Meantimes we shelter     place
our faith in sacraments of research     contact those we love

again     again     again     make pastry and poetry if we can
find the flour     fresh water     *le mot juste* to start

hope like anything that rises into what can be passed around
    Even as the blight demands to spread this minute

into months of loss     we persist because we have known
mercy in other dark hours and must attend to grace extended

Our lives are levain     Our love is vital     Our witness is steam

## Our Best Brains

Our best brains say we will get through this month,
one that will be chock full of fear, death, rage,
hell.  So far, we are still here as we cringe,
bear, breathe, laugh in odd new ways.  One more
day till we go to the store, and we're down
to last year's mac and cheese.  Some odd bent cans
at the backs of shelves are mixed with glops of
this weird spice, that freak herb, and we taste test
the dire hash till the gorge of each of us
does not rise much.  You tell me with a wink
*It's a feast.*  I flinch back a grin that says
*Like there's a choice?*  We make our list, we drive,
we mask and glove up, we buy what we need
for two more weeks.  We rest, read some, watch more
screen stuff than is wise.  We turn the next page
of the time frame we live in, and wait for
next month's best brains to kick in, keep us safe.

# Recollection

Perhaps
it is this

pair of wings
we once wore

making love,
taking the morning

as it arrived
in quicksilver grace,

grazing the trees,
whisking the waters,

until everything stirred,
everything stilled.

Later we gathered
the dry feathers

dropped during flight—
each one etched silver—

amazed how far
we had traveled

on only one pair
of shared wings.

Perhaps
it is this

shine remaining
after all such nights

sparkling inside
the pillowcases.

## *Garabato*

Scribble your way to me.  Pencil me in
by scrawling your way out of this blank space.
Ticonderoga or Sharpie shaved thin—
makes no matter.  Show me your voice and face

in your first-draft doodles, your John Keats curls
and whorls, Ulam spirals to show you're bored,
about to howl, to dance, a chance for swirls
beyond box step or borderline, a chord

played on strings of your creation.  Avail
yourself, involve me as your drafting desk,
allow your soul's slightest whim and detail,
depict a once and future arabesque,

a *geometría* of our free hands,
*una belleza* neither understands.

# Postcard from Lethe Valley

Dear Who You Are,

I know you, or the all of you that isn't the name others call you. Not that I've forgotten how you move or smile, and your words both fond and heinous. Where the ryegrass bent to our spring longing, I recollect entirely. I apprehend your silences all these years, and the furrows they have sown between us when I was too fearful to ask why.

We both drank our moments wholly, to the dregs, till we were bone white and frail, our ardor sluiced and sieved from us. Your face, my hands, how they enfolded each other. A wonder that I cannot recall the space between caresses. What we are this evening. Whenever I try. Wherefore. Used to know that. Can you repeat? Let me try whatever it is again. I will always reach, you know.

Love, Old What's-My-Name

# The Same

We kid ourselves: this is the same
porch, familiar white rail,

view of constant clouds, wind
brushing cedar boughs, eggs

breaking into red scrambling bowl
in the too-small kitchen.

The news, the news, the news
still tells us all is

war, craters, broken levees.
In the unabridged dictionary in the den,

*misery* still has the same letters, and
our dentist sends us happy yellow reminders

of our next hygiene appointment. Traffic
lights on our street are synchronized.

But the crow sits on a different branch
this morning, complaining

or bragging in a different timbre. The lawn
has a new fairy ring. Someone is singing

nearby. The old tune catches us by surprise.

# Acknowledgements

First, foremost, and indeed, I am everlastingly grateful to Susan for your love abounding and decades of support, encouragement, and tolerance. Graham and Mark, I treasure and thank you for the joy of being your dad. Great gratitude to Dina and Orly for your power and light.

I am indebted to all exemplary and practicing poets, songwriters, musicians, teachers, friends, theater folks, countless other wordplayers, metromaniacs, and other keepers of poetry's flame who have kept me saner than I'd be otherwise and more inspired than I've any right to.

Particular appreciation to William Stafford, Lucille Clifton, Naomi Shihab Nye, Wendell Berry, Jane Hirshfield, Joy Harjo, Kenneth Patchen, Lawrence Ferlinghetti, Denise Levertov, Pablo Neruda, Juan Felipe Herrera, W. S. Merwin, Mary Oliver, Gary Snyder, C. D. Wright, Lee Nicholson, Gillian Wegener, Lee Herrick, Maw Schein Win, Linda Toren, Linda Scheller, Stella Beratlis, Jill Harlan-Gran, Sheila Landre, Modesto-Stanislaus Poetry Center, my fellow Licensed Fools, the Curriculum Study Commission, The Community of Writers, First United Methodist Church, Prospect Theater Project, Robert Johnson, the Guthrie/Seeger/Dylan/Springsteen continuum, Chris Strachwitz, John Hartford, John Prine, Django Reinhardt, Leonard Cohen, Richard Thompson, Taj Mahal, Rhiannon Giddens, Chris Smither, Jason Isbell, Ray Davies, Mark Knopfler, Dave Brubeck, Charles Mingus, John Coltrane.

Very special thanks to Jack Sutton for his skill in photographing this old head and to Sara Stevenson for her splendid cover art.

Thanks, finally, to you reading this book; I am mighty beholden.

Grateful acknowledgement to the following publications in which these poems first appeared, sometimes in slightly different versions:

*California English:* "Even This Day"
*Comstock Review:* "Arrayed Like These"
*Collision: The Impact of Poetry and Photography:* "Ardea"
*Collision V: At the Intersection of Poetry and Photography:* "A Mercantile (Deleliquerat)"
*In the Grove:* "While Looking for Levee Breaks, He Leans on His Shovel and Does This—"

*More Than Soil*, More Than Sky: *The Modesto Poets:* "The Same"
*Snail Mail Review:* "After the Epithalamium"
*Stockton Arts Commission's Poetry Competition Anthology:* "Neruda and My Mother"

Gary Thomas grew up on a peach farm outside Empire, California. Prior to retirement, he taught eighth grade language arts for thirty-one years, and junior college English for seven, sharing and discussing at least one poem every day with his students. He has presented poetry workshops for statewide organizations, festivals, and conferences. He has had poems published in *California English, In the Grove, Time of Singing,* and *The Comstock* Review, among others, and in the anthologies *More Than Soil, More Than Sky: The Modesto Poets* and three of the *Collision* series. He is currently vice president of the Modesto-Stanislaus Poetry Center.

www.ingramcontent.com/pod-product-compliance
Lightning Source LLC
Chambersburg PA
CBHW021151090426
42740CB00008B/1044